THE POWER OF RELATIONSHIP CONSISTENCY

What It Means and Why It Matters

GINA CORTEZ

TABLE OF CONTENT

INTRODUCTION

Our lives are shaped by the consistent actions we take, not the occasional ones.

In order to succeed in business, life, and recreation, consistency is essential. I promise to follow through on what I claim I'll do. I'm assuming that since you are reading this, you also want to commit to doing this.

My own experience has shown that in order to develop trust, authenticity, and continue to expand success, consistency must be maintained over time. No matter what life throws at them, persistent folks never give up!

The main purpose of making excuses is to make yourself feel better while trying to avoid fulfilling your obligations.

But what is consistency in reality?

Perfect comes with practice. After a lot of practice, our work will become effortless, skilled, quick, and steady.

Be constant if you want to improve as a writer. Do you also want to slim down? Be consistent. Do you want to master anything? Next, act consistently.

Relationship consistency refers to a degree of predictability, reliability, and dependability. Couples may feel their relationship has progressed to a point of familiarity and comfort when utilized in a romantic context.

It can be difficult if things become stuck in a rut, but confidence and trust are also important ingredients. There is always someone accessible to strengthen, cheer on, inspire, and encourage when a support system is required.

Through regular dedication, availability, consistent daily communication, and getting to know one another, two people in a partnership have made the decision to be exclusive and have advanced to what it means to commit to each other.

The link solidifies as they get closer to one another.

CHAPTER ONE

Consistency

The meaning of Consistency in a relationship.

In a relationship, consistency is recurring conduct that fosters confidence and trust in each partner. When acting consistently, a partner will be on time when scheduling meetings and keep in touch frequently when the two of them are apart.

In a relationship, the desire to get to know one another comes first consistently and steadily. In what develops into an honest and exclusive partnership, each decides to spend meaningful time with the other.

Take a peek at this research to learn how consistency relates to commitment.

Why it is crucial for a relationship to be consistent.

In a relationship, consistency is vital because it denotes steadiness, responsibility, and honesty—basically, the cornerstones of a partnership. Relationships can foster growth and the formation of bonds as long as each party makes an effort to be consistent.

Since consistency requires conscious effort, it indicates a lack of desire to foster that connection if only one person is inconsistent. If you want to improve the behavior and establish consistency in a relationship, it also needs the same work.

What does consistency in a love affair look like?

Early on in a relationship, attraction, chemistry, and infatuation dominate thought and get a pair through the initial months of dating. However, as stability starts to take hold, continuous relationships are the telltale sign of true tenacity.

Love must endure as a pair becomes cosy, gets closer, and creates exclusivity. It's during this time that confidence and trust begin to develop.

What are some telltale signals that a partner is being reliable in a new relationship? Take a peek.

1. A contact- and time-based endeavor

Consistent partners will be generous with their time in a relationship. Each partner should be able to use that. One person shouldn't be exerting all the work.

Step back for a while to see if your partner tries to make some arrangements if you seem to be the one initiating making plans, setting up a time to spend together, or setting up dates.

It's also a good idea to go back over those dates and times to see if there was any inconsistent behavior in terms of showing up to any of the plans you made.

Aside from spending time together, consistency in a relationship includes checking in with each other on a regular basis. If you can't see each other for a few days, reach out with a phone call, video message, or other forms of communication.

2. Keeps promises

A love language that expresses dependability and reliability is consistency. A partner can rest comfortably and they will keep their vows to their spouse. Find out my personal opinion about the love language of consistency here.

How a partner views a constant partner is a worry for them. Breaking commitments will only disappoint a deeply loved partner, and it is the last thing a reliable person wants to do.

Being the one person, a significant other can rely on is of utmost importance. Letting them down is not a good idea.

3. Behavior is more important than words.

A partner that is consistent in a relationship backs up their words with actions. Words tend to go old after a relationship moves past the honeymoon stage and into a comfortable level.

However, reliable partners ensure that their actions match what they say to you, leaving no room for ambiguity.

Whereas if attempts weren't made, familiarity might have slowly eroded part of that genuineness over time.

4. Even keel

A level of consistency in a relationship is obtained when partners reach a point where there is a gradual and steady pace, even temperaments, no hot and cold, lashing out, or frustration directed at one another.

Someone who feels the need to vent about you (nearly daily) or who possibly offers conflicting signals, such as showing interest one minute and being distant the next, is probably not the perfect match for you.

5. Consistent

Predictability requires consistency. You'll be aware of what to anticipate from this mate. Some people might find that unappealing if they don't have that; nevertheless, the contrary is true.

Your comfort and security are eventually greatly increased by the repeated conduct, which you begin to value and adore. Regarding feelings, whether they care or have intentions, there is no doubt. You are aware of your situation and your importance.

6. Is sluggish

The majority of people that go through an infatuation and gregarious attraction phase with a consistent companion don't exactly go through your honeymoon phase.

These kinds of partnerships have a lot of inconsistencies, and occasionally they end abruptly.

When you are consistent in a relationship from the start, it almost feels comfortable, which allows for slow development.

In contrast to a powerful come-on at the beginning that would be on weak ground, this establishes a firmer framework for what could develop into exclusivity.

7. Friends and family

A partner that is dependable in a relationship will progressively incorporate you into their social and familial networks.

It's a sign that a significant relationship is growing and that your partner has a pattern of conduct in which they gradually introduce you to more and more elements of their life.

It doesn't matter if it's their house, their hobbies and interests, their job, or the people in their lives.

The next step in the relationship can be achieved by building a foundation of trust and confidence, which is probably what your partner is hoping for.

How you can maintain consistency in a relationship?

You should approach consistency in a relationship similar to how you would build trust and confidence with another individual because these two things are intertwined.

Being consistent in a relationship fosters trust, the ability to rely on your partner, and a sense of security in the union.

If there is a problem with your spouse, you must not only make sure you are being consistent but also figure out how to make him more so.

Here is some advice for maintaining consistency in a union.

1. Communicate

The most important thing in any relationship is to talk to each other, especially if something new has come up. Being consistent might be difficult, especially if neither of you has been practicing it.

In order to avoid disappointment for either party, you must first decide if the partnership is something you want to pursue to that extent.

2. Connection

Being constant in a relationship involves having regular, in-person contact.

That means making the most of uninterrupted, quality time spent together as often as you can. These instances will eventually result in a connection.

When you don't make time for each other or when your time together is complicated by electronics or other distractions, it can be difficult to connect.

3. If you don't mean it, don't say it.

Make sure what you say is something you truly believe. Being misled into thinking something is true is not pleasant. This breeds mistrust.

Then, when you do experience genuine emotion, the other person won't know how to interpret your gesture because your behavior has become consistent with being a phony.

This also applies when you claim to love something someone does for you but in reality, you don't.

Maybe you accidentally say you appreciate a particular food that your partner makes for you, but you later realize it wasn't your favorite. It's advantageous to admit that right away and without hesitation.

4. Adapt to needs

Your partner will see you as a solid source of support who they can turn to when they need you if you continuously make yourself accessible.

You can be someone who inspires them to pursue their goals, supports them when they get a work advancement or coaxes them out of their comfort zone to explore a new hobby.

Consistency also entails offering a shoulder to cry on in times of loss or adversity.

5. Follow-through

If you establish plans with your partner, be sure to keep your end of the bargain and don't back out at the last minute. The more you make promises and break them, the more your spouse will eventually start to distrust your word.

Being consistent in a relationship demonstrates your serious commitment to accountability and the fact that your spouse knows they can depend on you.

6. Sincere and Direct

A reliable partner is unfailingly honest. The person chooses to reveal any information their partner wants to know because they have nothing to hide.

No secrets or half-truths are wanted as the partnership moves forward; instead, a strong connection is preferred.

The connection can develop out of trust and respect when the partner of an honest, reliable mate is open and communicative.

7. Avoid habits you can't keep up

Contemplate whether you'll be able to continue a particular behavior or action when you consider it. If not, avoid the conduct because it will make you seem inconsistent and let others down.

Don't meet your friend for lunch if you believe it would be a nice idea but you won't be able to do it again since you'll be setting yourself up for the possibility that it will only happen seldom.

That applies to everyone. Every time someone does something novel or unexpected, we start to do it regularly.

8. Be Reliable.

Keep up the good work, be constant, and try not to let up when you see that your partner is appreciating your actions and the way the relationship is developing.

Too frequently, when things start to go well, we might become complacent. At that point, predictability, coziness, and familiarity converge with consistency. People do tend to repeat themselves. Really, it is very fantastic. Have faith in that.

But that doesn't imply you should stop making the consistent effort.

You must be dependable, stay in touch throughout the day, communicate, shower with intimacy, keep your word, and do everything else that keeps a relationship exciting and unique.

Without effort, "predictable" denotes that many people have negative associations. You become stuck. A connection must be consistent in order to succeed.

CHAPTER TWO

The Five Keys to Unlocking Consistency

Consistently repeat after me: CONSISTENT.

This word appears frequently in both written and spoken texts.

BUT what does this word actually mean?

In a nutshell, consistency is all about paying attention to the task at hand and being fully present at the moment. It kind of sounds like mindfulness. But what makes a difference is the background larger picture or the established goal.

When we do something regularly, we get feedback and start to perceive patterns. The change will result from this lesson. We will get better at something the more we practice it.

In other words, repetition is the definition of consistency. Through practice, we can become better over time, and some actions that may have started out as conscious effects can start to change into habits.

The Advantages of Regularity

There are numerous advantages to being more consistent in business, life, and even pleasure.

being able to measure

Better measurements are possible with consistency. For instance, unless you test something repeatedly, you won't know if it really works. Finding the right balance between spending enough time that you waste a lot of time if it doesn't work out is important for something to generate enough traction. This should last for three to six months before a review.

Consistency enhances reputation and trust.

The actual basis of trust is consistency. There is no point in speaking if you cannot keep your word.

Trust is developed with others at a steady pace. People know you're going to show up and perform. Consistent action requires an investment of time, trust, and reputation. People will become accustomed to, and even anticipate, your presence, and they may even seek your advice in areas where you "do your thing." How do you think this will appear if you only attend when you can be troubled?

Why is consistency such a challenge?

Although maintaining consistency seems like a straightforward idea, there are a lot of distractions around us, especially in modern culture, making it difficult to develop.

Additionally, some people simply lack the discipline, commitment, or focus necessary to persevere long enough to see results.

We are accustomed to instant gratification because of technologies like email, instant messaging, and same-day deliveries to the point that we fail to recognize that some things actually require time. Recall Rome? That wasn't constructed overnight, though.

Most of the time, if we don't immediately notice measurable outcomes, we don't see the sense in continuing. Consistency is more like a compound effect that creates gradual progress over time rather than about getting results quickly.

The Five keys to Consistency

These are the five keys I use to open the doors to my full potential, and I'm passing them along to you so you may open the doors to yours.

1. Make a timetable.

The hours will take care of themselves; therefore, I advise you to focus on the minutes.

Choose the times and dates that work for you and keep to them if you want to be consistent. Making a timetable means making sure you schedule time for breaks and your well-being in addition to the time you devote to a task. Consistency in taking breaks is just as crucial as consistency in completing chores.

2. Since motivation fades over time, self-control is essential.

People frequently claim that motivation is short-lived. Well, bathing doesn't either, which is why we advise doing it every day.

Motivation can give you the boost you need to get going, but self-discipline is necessary if you want to stick with it over the long haul. Although it's difficult, be strict with yourself. If you write, follow your timetable if you are a writer like me.

Plan at least two to three weeks ahead. Be prepared for any distractions in advance. They will occur; everyone will experience them. I'll utilize the Queen as my main illustration. She is reliable. She recently injured her back and had to postpone many royal engagements.

We were all caught off guard because we are accustomed to the Queen being devoted. Even with the finest plan, it's possible to occasionally forget a day. If that occurs, pick it up and don't be too hard on yourself. When a day suddenly turns into a week, a month, and eventually a year without any prior notice—and with no justification for your disappearance—that is when it becomes a problem.

3. Responsibility

You'll cluck if you hang out with chickens, and you'll fly if you hang out with eagles," the proverb goes.

Idealistically, you need a team to be consistent. a group that supports you, can hold you responsible for your behavior, and works to maintain your consistency However, you need to choose carefully.

Negative No Jo will sap your motivation and begin to attack your consistency. My friend, you must locate the eagles if you want to fly. People who act more and quack less are constantly looking for their next endeavor.

4. Persistence and Patience

Energy and perseverance overcome all obstacles.

If you put two people who are naturally gifted and persistent in the same room and watch them dance, chances are the persistent person will still be bopping long after the talented person has grown bored and left the room!

I've been writing for a long time—more than 10 years, to be exact—but it wasn't until recently that I received my first semi-viral article. Since then, though, several more of my tales have been successful. My perseverance and patience were finally rewarded.

5. Concentrate on one thing

Doing only one thing at a time is the fastest way to do many things.

Stick with any platform you choose for at least six months before switching to another if you want to succeed on it. It's simple to become a magpie searching for the next shiny object with so many social media platforms!

STOP, back up a step. Study up on the platform you are currently using. Only there should new content be published. You could reuse your main material there as well, linking back to "the one," if you do have numerous accounts.

Due to the structure of modern society, many people nowadays can be impatient. expecting quick outcomes without investing the time to become experts in their fields. It's an idealistic perspective.

True constancy for me as a writer does not, contrary to what some may have you believe, include writing every day. It's important to follow a set schedule, to be persistent and patient, and to feel at ease taking breaks. It may seem counterproductive, but if you don't schedule breaks, you'll quickly become exhausted.

It also involves having self-control and a commitment to turning up when you say you will. Finally, you need to locate those people who can hold you accountable for your activities. If you don't show up, call you, and extend your hand if you fall.

The door to becoming a top writer was opened for me by these five principles of constancy, which also support a healthy lifestyle. If I can use them, so can you.

CHAPTER THREE

How to improve Consistency

Your relationship lacks something.

That something is either physical intimacy or an emotional bond.

Perhaps you're dissatisfied and unhappy, and you're questioning the very foundations of your relationship with your partner.

While there might be a number of things that can go wrong in a committed, long-term relationship or marriage, problems with intimacy and connection are very common.

That doesn't make them any less painful to live through, but it does show that they can be overcome.

The truth is that many couples who struggle with a lack of physical or emotional intimacy at some point in their relationship manage to make things work in the long run.

They figure out how to rediscover and rebuild that bond.

You can, too.

What can you do to rekindle the spark in your relationship and reclaim some of the intimacy and connection that appears to have been lost?

The following steps can be taken to begin with:

1. Lower Your Expectations

That doesn't sound good, does it? It appears as if I'm telling you to accept the hand you've been dealt. That is not what I mean.

I don't mean to imply that your expectations should be low, but they should also not be unrealistically high.

It's important to remember that your physical relationship will almost certainly never have the same zeal that it did when you first met.

That's all due to pesky hormones, which go crazy when you first experience love and lust, but naturally settle down once you've transitioned into a committed relationship.

We wouldn't accomplish anything if we perpetually experienced the restlessness that comes with a new love.

You're setting yourself up for disappointment if you expect it to be as wild and passionate as it was when you first met.

You may have flashbacks to when you were first getting to know each other, and you'll continue to learn new things about each other as you both grow and your bodies and tastes change, but you can't expect your physical relationship to be earth-shattering for years.

It's also important not to let the media's popular notion (that if you don't have a revolutionary sex life, you're a failure) affect you.

You should aim for a physical relationship that makes you happy, based on a genuine connection with and understanding of your partner, rather than one that meets those ridiculous standards.

You should also maintain realistic expectations of emotional intimacy, as some people find that type of connection more difficult than others.

Though this is not always the case, men generally find emotional intimacy more difficult than women.

Understanding and accepting this to some extent will allow you to be more reasonable in your beliefs about what constitutes an intimate relationship.

2. Discuss it

I know you already understand the importance of communication, but when it comes to sensitive topics like sex, you may have hoped that you wouldn't have to sit down and have the big talk about it.

The first step in resolving the issue, however, really entails sitting down and talking about how you've been feeling regarding the physical intimacy and connection in your relationship.

You need to know that you and your partner are on the same page, that neither of you is blaming the other, and that you are both committed to working on it.

It's critical to never have this conversation after you've been intimate with each other, because that's when you're both feeling vulnerable and, with all those hormones rushing around, emotions can easily run high.

3. Consult with A Therapist

Sometimes a couple's communication skills aren't quite up to the task of simply sitting down and talking about their problems.

In many cases, having a third-party present can assist in resolving issues that a man and woman (or any combination thereof) may be experiencing.

A relationship or sex therapist can direct the conversation to the most important issues, keep things on track if they veer off track, and act as a mediator if disagreements arise.

They can also offer specific advice to address any issues that a couple may be experiencing.

Often, multiple sessions over a period of time are required, but the results often justify the investment.

4. Begin Small

Sex is only one aspect of physical intimacy. Holding hands, making proper eye contact, touching their arm, or hugging are all equally, if not more, important.

It's the small gestures you make on a daily basis that show your partner how much you care and keep the connection strong.

5. Become Romantic

Romance isn't all about grand gestures. It's about enjoying the beauty of life while also enjoying each other's company.

As busy as I'm sure you are, it's important to make time for each other and show your partner that you've put some thought into it.

Spend a little extra time preparing a special meal for them just because. Think creatively and outside the box. Take your partner on a picnic to a scenic location. Take in the sunset. Show them that you enjoy spending time with them and want to make memories.

6. Change Your Routine

These romantic gesture examples are just a few of the many ways you can break the cycle of your life.

A routine has many advantages, especially when life is hectic with children or other responsibilities.

A routine, on the other hand, allows you to coast through life without really paying attention to what's going on. It's a kind of autopilot.

In a relationship, you may not even notice that emotional and physical intimacy has dwindled.

So, take advantage of as many opportunities as you can to break out of your routine and try something new and different. Or, at the very least, things you don't do very often.

Visit new places, try new activities as a couple, meet new people, broaden your cultural horizons...

...do anything that will make you and your partner notice each other again, rather than drifting through life as mere co-passengers.

When you break free from the monotony of a routine-driven life, emotional intimacy will return.

7. Separate Things

As much as trying new things together can bring you closer together, you should also take some time apart.

This is especially useful if you and your partner spend the majority of your free time together. You may believe that this is a sign of a loving relationship, but having space and freedom to pursue your own interests is essential for each person's emotional well-being.

It allows you to miss each other and appreciate what you have when you return to it.

It also relieves the pressure of constantly being in each other's pockets.

8. Be the first to open the door

When one partner begins to close off his or her emotions, the other often follows suit.

It's an almost instinctive reaction. We tend to mirror those around us, so if our partner gives less emotionally, we tend to give less emotionally in return.

The same is true for any form of emotional expression (or non-expression). Anger breeds more anger. Joy spreads like wildfire. Sadness feeds on itself.

The solution is to re-open yourself and allow your partner to see and mirror you.

You must break down any barriers you have erected and continue to express your emotions and love for them as much as possible.

Your partner will feel less anxious about the relationship and more able to open up again if you offer them your emotional warmth.

Create a safe space for your partner to truly be themselves in your presence, and emotional intimacy and connection will naturally follow.

This almost always leads to increased physical intimacy.

9. Be encouraging and supportive.

When your partner shows signs of vulnerability by expressing emotions or opening up in some other way, show your appreciation and be completely positive about the experience.

Your partner must understand that you will be there for them no matter how difficult the process is.

The more they realize they are not alone in this, and the more secure they feel in opening up, the further they will push their emotional boundaries.

Allow them to move at their own pace. It will take some time for them to gain enough confidence in their ability to be emotionally close to you if they have been emotionally withdrawn for a long time or for as long as you have known them.

10. Look After Yourself

With advertising and Instagram, there's a lot of pressure to look a certain way in the modern world, and I'm not going to add to that.

Beauty isn't one-size-fits-all, and you shouldn't try to meet unrealistic expectations.

However, rejecting beauty standards does not preclude you from caring for yourself.

Taking a little extra care with your appearance and personal grooming can make a big difference because if you don't feel attractive, you're likely to transmit that to your partner.

After all, as we've all heard, it's difficult to accept love from others if you don't love yourself.

Do things that make you happy, whether it's as simple as taking time for yourself, taking a bath, booking a spa day, eating food that nourishes you and leaves you feeling energized, or exercising in a way that makes you feel fantastic.

Fit comes in all shapes and sizes, so exercise isn't about achieving a specific body type. Exercising means you'll have more energy and a more positive outlook on life, which is appealing to anyone.

When you look in the mirror, focus on what you like rather than what you want to change.

Simultaneously, support your partner when they do things for themselves and don't forget to tell them how beautiful they are on the inside and out.

11. De-stress

When you are continually checking your work emails or are preoccupied with the mountain of work that will be waiting for you the next morning, it might be difficult to connect with your partner.

Your partner probably knows you better than anyone else, so they'll be able to tell when you're not really in the room with them.

When you are not stressed, all aspects of your life will improve, not just your relationship with your partner. You ought to give it maximum importance.

Exercising helps you de-stress, and finding an activity that helps you calm your hectic mind, whether it's yoga, journaling, meditation, or simply reading a good book, can help.

You owe it to your partner to be fully present and give them the attention they deserve when you're with them.

12. Don't Expect Change to Happen Overnight

Those who wait will be rewarded. Make a concerted effort to implement the suggestions above in your relationship, but don't expect immediate results. With time and patience, the intimacy you seek will bloom once more.

And you'll most likely discover that one type of intimacy leads to another. So, if it's easier to start with the more physical aspects of things (and we're not just talking about sex), go for it.

Alternatively, if you want to address the physical distance between you first, growing the emotional side of things should work as well.

CHAPTER FOUR

CONCLUSION

When you get your groove together, stability in a relationship takes time and effort to develop. Since they're still in the honeymoon period and need to see each other frequently, some couples start out with some consistency.

The absolute consistency, however, doesn't appear when you start with a powerful come-on that is more focused on infatuation until some realism starts to sink in.

It's impossible to fully learn consistency from someone else. It's a rhythm that you and your spouse establish together.

But if you and your spouse are having trouble getting there on your own, especially if you sincerely want to work on that together, a counsellor can point you in the right direction.

www.ingramcontent.com/pod-product-compliance
Lightning Source LLC
LaVergne TN
LVHW052110160826
845678LV00015B/3477

* 9 7 9 8 3 5 2 4 8 8 9 6 6 *